MW01171823

## Introduction

Bar-Nava, the Son of Comfort, is mentioned in Ma'aseh Shlichim/Acts 1:23, 4:36, 9:27, 11:22, 25, 30, 12:25, 13:1, 2, 7, 43, 46, 50, 14:12, 14, 20, 15:2, 12, 22, 25, 35, 36, 37, 39, Qorintyah Alef/1st Corinthians 9:6, Galutyah/Galatians 2:1, 9, 13, and in Qolesayah/Colossians 4:10. From these biblical references we can see concerning Bar-Nava that:

-He was a traveling companion Of Rav Shaul/Paul.
-He introduced Rav Shaul/Paul to the Jerusalem community of faith.
-He was trusted by the Jerusalem elders. He was faithful with finances.
-He was a Jewish believer. He was A Levite.

*-His Hebrew name was Yoseph/Joseph.*
*-He was a missionary and had a pastor's heart. He was considered a teacher and a prophet.*
*-He was ordained by the Ruach HaKodesh/Holy Spirit to rescue Ephraim from the nations.*
*-He was from the island of Cyprus.*
*-He observed Shabbat with the Jewish people.*
*-He was a key speaker and delegate at the Acts 15 Jerusalem Council.*
*-He was a chosen ambassador by the Jerusalem Council sent out with their rulings.*
*-He continued secular work.*
*-He was rebuked by Paul for following Peter in withdrawing from table fellowship from returning Ephraimites. This is a second issue where he is seen in sharp disagreement with Paul.*
*-He had a sharp break in fellowship with Rav Shaul/Paul. He was a believer before Paul.*
*-He donated large amounts of land and other material needs to the early Nazarene Yisraelite community.*
*-His nephew was Yochanan Moshe/John Mark author of the gospel bearing his name. Moshe-Markus was a visitor when Paul was in prison in Rome.*

The Epistle of Barnabas-Bar-Nava is a Greek treatise with some features of an epistle containing twenty-one chapters, preserved complete in the 4th century Codex Sinaiticus where it appears at the end of the Renewed Covenant/New Testament. It is traditionally ascribed to the Barnabas-Bar- Nava who is mentioned in the Acts of the Apostles, though some ascribe it to another apostolic father of the same name, a "Barnabas-Bar-Nava of Alexandria," or simply attribute it to an unknown early Nazarene Yisraelite teacher. A form of the Epistle 850 lines long is noted in the Latin list of canonical works in the 6th century Codex Claromontanus. It is not to be confused with the Gospel of Barnabas-Bar-Nava.

The ancient writers who refer to this Epistle unanimously attribute it to Barnabas-Bar-Nava the Levite, of Cyprus, who held an honorable place in the infant assembly. Clement of Alexandria does so again and again (Strom, ii. 6, ii. 7, etc.). Origen describes it as "a Universal Epistle" (Cont. Cels, i. 63), and seems to rank it among the Sacred Scriptures (Comm. in Rom., i. 24). Other statements have been quoted from the fathers, to show that they held this to be an authentic production of the apostolic Barnabas-Bar-Nava; and certainly no other name is ever hinted at in Nazarene Yisraelite antiquity as that of the writer.

It was clearly written after the destruction of Jerusalem, since reference is made to that event (chap. 16.), but how long after is a matter of much dispute. The general opinion is, that its date is not later than the middle of the second century and that it cannot be placed earlier than some twenty or thirty years before. The intention of the writer, as he himself states (chap. 1), was "to perfect the knowledge" of those to whom he wrote.

Until the recent discovery of the Codex Sinaiticus by Tischendorf, the first four and a half chapters were known only in an ancient Latin version. The whole Greek text is now happily recovered, though it is in many places very corrupt.
Generally, the skeptics who feel that The Epistle of Barnabas-Bar-Nava is anti Torah and antinomian in its context are simply following ancient post Nicene century opinions. Remember, Eusebius was chief author of the Nicene Creed and also wanted Revelation, Jude, James and any other Hebraic Nazarene Yisraelite writings out of the canon, as they seemed to him and others as being "too Jewish."
*The Epistle* is included in the earliest Greek versions of the Renewed Covenant (including the *Sinaiticus* - 3rd century). It is Hebraic in character and explains several hidden meanings of the Hebrew Scriptures, including the higher meaning of sacrifices, food ordinances, the 8-day prophetic week and what it really means to be a Nazarene Yisraelite.

This letter was originally written by the Apostle Bar-Nava, who split from Paul - and besides the Hebraic character of the letter - this might be the true reason it was finally *excluded from the canon*.

CODEX SINAITICUS: The New Testament translated from the Sinaitic Manuscript. Discovered by Constantine Tischendorf at Mt.

Sinai (the false one) by H. T. Anderson Translated by Charles Hoole, 1885.

## Barnabas-Bar-Nava 1

## Barnabas-Bar-Nava 1

1  Hail, my sons and daughters *in Yisrael*, in the name of our Adon Yahusha the Messiah, who has loved us in shalom.

2  I rejoice exceedingly and beyond measure at your happy and glorious ruach, since the ordinances of the Torah of Elohim are great and rich towards you, who have received the engrafted unmerited favor of the spiritual gift.

3  Wherefore, I congratulate myself the more, hoping to be saved, because I see of a truth the Ruach poured out upon you from the rich Elohim of love. So greatly has your longed-for appearance hit me with amazement.

4  Being persuaded, therefore, of this, and knowing in myself that since I spoke among you, YHUH has helped me in many things in the way of righteousness. I am altogether compelled to love you even beyond my own soul, because great emunah and love dwells in you, in the hope of His chayim.

5  Considering also this, that if I take care to communicate to you a part of that which I have received, it shall turn to my reward to have assisted such spirits as you are, I gave diligence to write unto you in few words, in order that together with your emunah, you might have your knowledge perfect also.

6  For there are three doctrines ordained of YHUH: the hope of

chayim, the beginning, and the end.

7  For the Master has made known unto us by the prophets the things that are past, and the things, which are at hand, and has given us the bikkurim/firstfruits of the knowledge of the things that are to come. Since, therefore, we see all these things each working as He has spoken, we ought the more fully and royally approach His altar;

8  But I, not as a teacher, but as one of yourselves, will show to you a few things, by means of which you may even in this present rejoice.

---

## Barnabas-Bar-Nava 2

1   Since, therefore, the days are evil, and the adversary has the authority, we ought to take heed to ourselves and seek out the Torah of YHUH.

2   For the helpers of our emunah are reverence and patience, and they that fight on our side are long-suffering and continence.

3   While these, therefore, remain pure in things relating to YHUH, wisdom and understanding, science and knowledge, rejoice together with them.

4   For Elohim has made known unto us through all the prophets, that He desires neither sacrifices nor whole burnt offerings, nor oblations; for He said in a certain place,

5   To what purpose is the multitude of your sacrifices? said YHUH. I am full of the whole burnt offerings of rams; I desire not the fat of lambs, nor the blood of bulls and goats, nor need you come to be seen of Me. For who has required these things at your hands? You shall not add thereto to tread my court. If you bring the fine flour, it is vain; incense is an abomination unto me; your new moons and Shabbats I cannot endure; your fastings and holidays and moadim my soul hates.

6   These things, therefore, He has made of none effect, that the new instructions of our Adon Yahusha the Messiah, being free from the yoke of necessity,  might have an offering not made with hands.

7   Again, He said unto them, Did I command your ahvot/fathers, when you came out of the land of Mitzrayim, to offer unto me whole burnt offerings and sacrifices?

8   Did I not rather command them this? – Let each of you bear no malice against his neighbor in his heart, and love not a false oath.

9   We ought to perceive, since we are not void of understanding the meaning of the goodness of Elohim our Father, because He

tells us, wishing to seek us who are wandering even as sheep, how we ought to approach Him.

10   He therefore speaks unto us in this way: The sacrifice before Elohim is a broken heart; a smell of sweet savor unto YHUH is a heart that glorifies Him that made it. We ought, therefore, brethren, to examine accurately concerning our salvation, lest the evil one, making an entrance among us, should draw us away from our chayim.

_____

## Barnabas-Bar-Nava 3

1 Therefore, He said again, concerning these things, unto them. Why do you fast unto me, said YHUH, so that your voice is heard today in its crying? This is not the fast that I have chosen, said YHUH, for a man to humiliate his soul;

2 Nor if you bend your neck as a ring, and put under you sackcloth and ashes – not even then will you call it an acceptable fast.

3 But unto us He said, Behold the fast which I have chosen, said YHUH; not that a man should humiliate his soul, but that he should loose every bond of unrighteousness, and untie the knots of the compacts of violence; set at liberty them that are bruised, and cancel every agreement of unrighteousness; break your bread with the hungry, and if you see the naked, clothe him; bring them that are homeless into your dwelling, and if you see a man that is lowly, despise him not, and turn not away from those of your family;

4 Then shall your light break forth early, and your garments shall spring up quickly, and justice shall go before you, and the glory of YHUH shall surround you;

5 Then shall you cry, and YHUH shall listen unto you; while you are yet speaking He shall say, See, I am here: if you put away from you the league and the conspiracy, and the word of murmuring, and give your bread to the hungry with all your heart, and have compassion upon the soul that is lowly.

6 The long-suffering Elohim therefore having seen beforehand that the people whom He had prepared for His beloved would believe in simplicity, showed to us beforehand concerning all these things, that we should not come as strangers to their Torah.

## Barnabas-Bar-Nava 4

1   It behooves, therefore, that we, searching much concerning the things that are at hand, should seek out the things that are able to save us. Let us flee, therefore, utterly from all the work of unrighteousness, and let us hate the error of the time that now is, that we may be loved in that age which is to come.

2   Let us not give liberty unto our soul that it should have leave to run with sinners and evil men, neither let us be made like unto them.

3   The Tribulation being made perfect is at hand, concerning which it is written, as Enoch said, For to this purpose YHUH has cut short the times and the days, that His beloved might make haste and come into His inheritance.

4   The prophet also speaks in this way: Ten kingdoms shall reign upon the earth; and there shall rise up after them a little king who shall humble three of the kings under one.[6]

5   And in like manner Daneiyel/Daniel speaks concerning him: And I saw the fourth beast, evil and strong and harder than all the beasts of the earth; and I saw how there grew up from him ten horns, and from among them a little horn, growing up beside them, and how it humbled under one three of the great horns.

6   You ought, therefore, to understand. And moreover I ask this of you, as being one among you, loving you especially and altogether, even above my own soul; that you should take heed unto yourselves, and not be like unto certain men, by adding to your sins and saying that their covenant is also ours. Ours, indeed, it is; but they have lost it forever, in this way, after that Moshe had already received it.

7   For the Scripture said, And Moshe was in the mount fasting forty days and nights, and he received the covenant from YHUH; even tables of stone written with the finger of the hand of YHUH. But when they turned unto idols they lost it.

8   For YHUH said this unto Moshe, Moshe, get down quickly, for your people, whom you brought out of the land of Mitzrayim, have done unlawfully. And Moshe understood, and cast the two tables from his hands, and the covenant that was on them was broken; to the end that that of the beloved Yahusha might be sealed in our hearts in the hope of His emunah.

9   Now, though I wished to write many things unto you, not as a teacher, but even as fits one that loves you, not to fall short of the things that we have, I have been zealous to write unto you as though I were the off scouring of you. Let us, therefore, give heed unto the last days; for the whole time of our emunah will profit us nothing unless now, in the season of iniquity and among the stumbling-blocks that are coming, we resist as becomes the sons of Elohim,

10   That the evil one may not have entrance unawares. Let us fly away from all vanity and hate perfectly the deeds of the evil way. Do not, entering into your own houses, dwell alone, as though you were already justified, but coming together, inquire one with another concerning the common advantage.

11   For the Scripture said, Woe unto them that are wise in their own conceit and learned in their own eyes. Let us be spiritual: let us be a perfect Temple unto Elohim. So far as in you lies, let us practice the reverence of Elohim, and strive to keep His Torah commandments, that we may be glad in His ordinances.

12   YHUH shall judge the world without respect of persons; each shall receive according as he has done; if he is tov/good, righteousness shall go before him, but if he is evil, the reward of wickedness shall be before him.

13   Let us give heed that we do not, as being already elect, take rest, and sleep in our sins, lest the ruler of wickedness, getting the mastery over us, thrust us from the kingdom of YHUH.

14   And, moreover, my brethren, consider this. When you see that after so many signs and wonders what has happened to Yisrael, even then they have been abandoned for now; let us take

heed lest, as it is written, many of us be called but few chosen.

—————————————————

## Barnabas-Bar-Nava 5

1 For on this account YHUH endured to give His flesh unto corruption, that we might be sanctified by the remission of sins, which is by the sprinkling of His blood.

2 For there are written concerning Him certain things that pertain unto Yisrael, and certain others that pertain unto us. For He speaks thus, He was wounded for our iniquities, and vexed for our sins; by His stripes we are healed. He was led as a sheep unto the slaughter, and like a Lamb dumb before him that shears it.

3 We ought therefore, to give special thanks unto YHUH because He has made known unto us the things that are past, and has made us wise with regard to those that are at hand, neither are we without understanding as regards to the future.

4 For the Scripture said, Not unjustly is the net stretched for the birds. Now this means that a man will perish justly who, having knowledge of the path of righteousness, shuts himself up into the way of darkness.

5 Consider this too, my brethren; if YHUH endured to suffer for our souls, though He were YHUH of the whole world, to whom Elohim said from the foundation of the world, Let us make man according to our image and according to our likeness, how then did He endure to suffer at the hands of men? Learn!

6 The prophets having received the unmerited favor from Him and prophesied with regard to Him. But He, that He might make death of none effect and bring to light the resurrection from the dead, because it behooved Him to be made manifest in the flesh,

7 Endured it that He might give unto our ahvot/fathers the promise, and by preparing for Himself a renewed people might show, while upon earth, that He will raise the dead and by Himself execute judgment.

8 Yes, further; though He taught Yisrael and did so many signs and wonders among them, yet they loved Him not.

9   But when He chose out His own Apostles, who were about to preach His Besorah/gospel, they were men unrighteous beyond all sin, that He might show that He came not to call the righteous, but sinners to repentance; then He made Himself manifest that He was the Son of Elohim.

10   For if He had not come in the flesh how could men have looked upon Him and have been saved, since they cannot endure to look at the rays of the sun which must one day perish, and which is the work of His hands?

11   For this purpose did the Son of Elohim come in the flesh, that He might sum up and finish the sin of them who persecuted His prophets unto death;

12   Therefore He endured even unto this. For Elohim said that the smiting of His flesh it was from them. When they shall smite their Shepherd, then shall the sheep of the flock be scattered.

13   But He himself wished thus to suffer, for it was necessary that He should suffer upon the execution stake; for He who prophesied about Him said, Spare my soul from the sword, and again, Drive nails into My flesh, for the synagogues of evil men have risen against Me.

14   And again He said, Behold, I have given My back unto the scourging and My cheeks unto buffetings; My face also have I set as a hard rock.

---

## Barnabas-Bar-Nava 6

1   When, therefore, He made the Torah what said He? Who is he that disputes with Me? Let him resist Me; or who is he that contends with Me? Let him draw near unto the Son of YHUH.

2   Woe unto you, for you shall all wax old as a garment, and the moth shall devour you. And again the prophet said, Since He has been placed, as a strong Stone, for crushing; behold I will place on the foundation of Tzion, a stone precious, elect, a chief corner stone of great price.

3   And then what said he? And he that believeth in Him shall live forever. Is then our hope in a Stone? Elohim forbid. But it is thus said because YHUH has made strong His flesh, for He said, And He made Me as it were a hard Rock.

4   And again, The Stone, which the builders rejected, has become the head of the corner. And again He said, This is the day, great and wonderful, which YHUH has made.

5   I write unto you more simply that you may understand. I am the outcast of your love.

6   What then said the prophet again? The assembly of the wicked came around Me; they surrounded me as bees do a honeycomb, and, over My garment they cast lots.

7   Since, therefore, He was about to be made manifest and to suffer in the flesh, His suffering was shown beforehand. For the prophet said unto Yisrael, Woe unto their soul, for they have counseled an evil counsel among themselves, saying, Let us bind the righteous because He is an encumbrance unto us.
8   And what said the other prophet, even Moshe, unto them? Behold, thus says YHUH Elohim: Enter into the tov/good land, which YHUH swore unto Avraham/Abraham and Yitzchak/Isaac and Yaakov/Jacob, and inherit it, even a land flowing with milk and honey.

9   What said knowledge? Learn it. Hope, it said, upon Yahusha, who is about to be manifested unto you in the flesh. For man is

but earth, which suffers; for, from the face of the ground was made the molding for Adam.

10   What then means He when He said, In to the tov/good land which flows with milk and honey? Blessed be YHUH, brethren, who has put into you wisdom and knowledge of his secret things. For the prophet speaks a parable from YHUH. Who shall understand, except he that is wise and skilful and that loves his YHUH?

11   Since, therefore, having renewed us by the remission of our sins, He has made us of a new character; He wills that we should have the souls of children, inasmuch as it is indeed He who has formed us anew.

12   For the Scripture said concerning us, that He said unto the Son, Let us make man after our own image and according to our likeness; and let them rule over the beasts of the earth, and the fowls of heaven, and the fishes of the sea. And YHUH said, when He saw how excellent our form was, Increase and multiply and replenish the earth. These things he said unto the Son.

13   Again I will show unto you how YHUH speaks unto us, since He has made a second fashioning in these last days; YHUH said, Behold I make the last even as the first. For to this purpose did the prophet preach. Enter into the land flowing with milk and honey, and have dominion over it.

14   Behold now we have been formed again, even as He said again in another prophet: Behold, said YHUH, I will take out from these, that is out of those whom the Ruach of YHUH foresaw, the hearts of stone, and will put into them hearts of flesh, because He himself was about to be manifested in the flesh and to dwell among us.

15      For the habitation of our heart is a Temple holy unto YHUH.

16   For Yahusha said again, Whereby shall I appear before YHUH my Elohim and be glorified? He said too, I will give thanks unto

You in the assembly, in the midst of My brethren; I will sing unto You in the midst of the assembly of the saints. We are, therefore, those whom He brought into the tov/good land.

17   What, then, means the milk and honey? It is because a child is kept alive, first with honey, afterwards with milk. So we, too, being quickened by emunah in His promise and by His word, shall live and rule over the earth.

18   And we said previously, And let them increase and multiply and rule over the fish. Who then is he who is able to rule over the beasts, the fish, and fowls of heaven? For we ought to perceive that to rule means authority, so that a man by giving commands may exercise lordship.

19   If, therefore, this does not take place now, He has told us when it will; even when we ourselves have been made perfect, so that we become heirs of the covenant of YHUH.

_____

## Barnabas-Bar-Nava 7

1   You perceive, therefore, beloved children that our tov/good YHUH has manifested unto us all things beforehand, to the end that we should know whom we ought to praise, returning thanks for all things.

2   If, therefore, the Son of Elohim, being He who is YHUH  and who is about to judge the living and the dead, suffered, to the end that His stripes might make us live, let us believe that the Son of Elohim could not suffer except on our account.
3   But being crucified, He was given to drink of vinegar and gall. How, then, did the priests of the temple signify concerning this? Now, the commandment is written this way: Whosoever shall not fast on the fast, he shall die the death; YHUH has commanded it. Since He also was about to offer the vessel that contained His ruach as a sacrifice, in order that the type might be fulfilled which was given by the offering of Yitzchak/Isaac at the altar,

4   What said He in the book of the prophet? And let them eat of the goat, which is offered on the fast for the sins of all. Attend diligently to this. And let the priests alone eat of the unwashed intestines with vinegar.

5   What is the significance? Because you will one day give Me to drink of vinegar and gall, when I am about to offer up My flesh for My renewed people, you eat it alone, while the people fast and lament in sackcloth and ashes. He commanded this in order that He might show that He needs to suffer at their hands.

6   How, then, did he give His commands? Listen! Take two goats, fair and like each other, and offer them up. And let the priest take one of them as a whole ascension offering for sin.

7   But what shall they do with the other? Let the other, He said, be accursed. Now listen, how the type of Yahusha is made manifest.

8   And do you not all spit upon it and pierce it, and put scarlet wool around its head, and so let it be cast out into the wilderness. And when this has been done, he who bears the goat leads it out

into the wilderness, and takes away the wool and places it upon a bush, which is called Rachel, the shoots of which we are accustomed to eat when we find them in the fields. Thus the fruit of the Rachel only is sweet.

9   What, therefore, means this? Listen! One is brought to the altar, the other is accursed, and the accursed one is crowned, because they shall see Him in that day, who had the scarlet robe about His flesh, and they shall say, Is not this He whom once we set at naught and crucified, and spat upon and pierced? Truly this was He who at that time said that He was the Son of Elohim.
10   How then was one like the other? In this respect were the goats like Him: they were fair and equal, so that when they saw Him coming they were astonished at the likeness to the goat. Therefore, behold here the type of Yahusha, who was about to suffer.

11   And what means the wool placed in the midst of thorns? It is a type of Yahusha, which has been placed in the assembly of Yisrael. For He who wishes to take the scarlet wool must suffer many things, because the thorn is terrible and sharp, and must only after pain gain possession of it. So He said, Those who wish to see Me and to take hold of My kingdom must through trouble and suffering receive Me.

---

## Barnabas-Bar-Nava 8

1   And what type, do you think, was the commandment unto Yisrael, that the men in whom sin had been accomplished should offer a heifer; and after they had slaughtered it should burn it; and that children should then take the ashes and cast them into vessels, and place scarlet wool and hyssop around a stick? Behold, again, the type of the execution stake and the scarlet wool – and so the children should sprinkle the people one by one, that they might be purged from their sins.

2   Behold, therefore, in what way He speaks unto you with simplicity. The red heifer signifies Yahusha; the sinful men who offer it are the men who brought Him unto the slaughter. But now the men are no longer before us, no longer does the glory belong to sinners.

3   The children who sprinkled the blood are they who brought us the Good News of the forgiveness of sins and purification of heart, to whom He has given the authority of the Good News for the purpose of preaching, being twelve in number, for a testimony unto the tribes, for twelve, were the tribes of Yisrael.

4   And why, then, were the children who sprinkled three in number? For a testimony unto Avraham/Abraham, Yitzchak/Isaac, and Yaakov/Jacob, because these are great before Elohim.
5   And what signifies the wool upon the stick? Because the kingdom of Yahusha is upon the execution stake; and because they who hope upon Him shall live forever.

6   And why are there at the same time the wool and the hyssop? Because in His kingdom, the days in which we shall be saved shall be evil and filthy; because also he that grieves over His flesh, is healed through the purifying of the hyssop.

7   And these things having happened on this account are manifest unto us, but obscure unto them, because they hearkened not unto the voice of YHUH.

## Barnabas-Bar-Nava 9

1   He said also again concerning our ears how he has circumcised our heart. YHUH said in the prophet, They have hearkened unto Me with the hearing of their ears; and again, He said, They that are far off shall hear with their ears; they shall know what I have done; and be circumcised, said YHUH, in your heart;

2   And again, Hear, O Yisrael/Shema Yisrael, for thus said YHUH your Elohim; and again the Ruach of YHUH prophesied, Who is he that wishes to live forever? Let him listen unto the voice of My Son.

3   And again He said, Hear, O heaven, and give ear, O earth, for YHUH has spoken these things for a testimony. And again He said, Listen unto the voice of YHUH, you rulers of this people. And again He said, Listen you children unto the voice of one crying in the wilderness.

4   To this end, therefore, has He circumcised our hearing, that when we hear His word, we should believe; for the circumcision in which they trust is done away with. For He has said that circumcision is not that which was made in the flesh; but they have transgressed, for an evil angel/malach has deluded them. [27]

5   He said unto them, These things said YHUH your Elohim – here I find a new commandment – Sow not among thorns, but be circumcised unto your YHUH. And what said He? Circumcise the hardness of your hearts, and harden not your neck. And again, Behold, said YHUH, all the nations are uncircumcised in their foreskin, but this nation is uncircumcised in their hearts.

6   But he will say, Of a truth the people have been circumcised for a seal unto them; but so, also, has every Syrian and Arabian, and all the priests of idols. Do they also belong to the covenant? But the Egyptians also are in circumcision. [28]

7   Learn, therefore, children of love, richly concerning all things; that Avraham, who first gave circumcision, circumcised, looking forward in the ruach unto Yahusha, having received the doctrines

of the three letters.

8   For he said, And Avraham circumcised out of his household eighteen souls and three hundred souls. What, then, is the knowledge that was given by this? Learn that he mentions the eighteen first, and then, having made a pause, he mentions the three hundred souls. In the eighteen, IH- YAH*, you have Yahusha; and because the execution stake in the letter Tau was about to convey the unmerited favor of redemption; He mentions also the three hundred. Therefore, he shows Yahusha in the two letters, IH-YAH and the execution stake in the one, T.

*That is, Iota and Eta and T [The doctrine of the three letters].

9   He knows this who has placed the engrafted gift of His teaching in us. No one has had from me a more true account than this; but I know that you are worthy.

_____

## Barnabas-Bar-Nava 10

1  But in that Moshe said, You shall not eat the swine, or the eagle, or the hawk, or the crow, or any fish that has no scales in itself, he had in his mind three doctrines.

2  For in the end he said unto them in Deuteronomy/Devarim, And I will arrange before this people my ordinances. The commandment of Elohim is not, therefore, that they should not eat; but Moshe spoke in a spiritual sense.
3  He spoke of the swine with this meaning: You shall not cleave, He means, unto men of this sort, who are like unto swine, for when they become filled up they forget their YHUH, but when they are in want they think upon YHUH; even as the swine when it eats knows not its Elohim, but when it is hungry it cries, and when it has received food it is again silent.

4  Nor shall you eat of the eagle, nor of the hawk, nor of the kite, nor of the crow. You shall not, He means, cleave not to, nor be like to men of this sort, who know not how to provide sustenance for themselves by labor and sweat, but in their iniquity seize the property of others, and, as though they walked in innocence, watch and observe whom they shall plunder, through their covetousness; even as these birds alone provide not sustenance for themselves by means of toil, but, sitting idle, seek out how they may eat the flesh of others, being destructive by reason of their wickedness.

5  And you shall not eat, he said, of the lamprey, or the polypus, or the cuttle-fish. You shall not, He means, cleave not to, or become like unto men of this sort, who are impious unto the end, and have been already condemned to death, even as these accursed fish alone swim in the depth, not floating as the others do, but dwelling in the earth below the depth of the sea.

6  Thus, he said, You shall not eat the hare, meaning you shall not indulge in unnatural lusts;

7      Nor shall you eat the hyena, meaning you shall not be an adulterer;

8  Nor shall you eat the weasel, meaning you shall not do uncleanness with your mouth concerning food;

9  Therefore Moshe spoke in the ruach these three doctrines. But they, according to the lusts of their flesh, received them as being only about meat.

10  And David receives knowledge concerning the same three doctrines, and said in like manner, Blessed is the man who has not walked in the counsel of the unrighteous, even as the unclean fish walk in darkness into the depths of the sea, and has not stood in the way of sinners, even as the unclean who pretend to fear YHUH sin as does the swine, and has not sat in the seat of the destroyers, even as the unclean birds that do sit for prey. You have also in the end a commandment concerning food;

11  But Moshe said, Eat everything that is cloven-footed and that chews the cud. What means he?

He that takes food knows him that feeds him, and, resting upon him, seems to be glad. He therefore said well, having regard to the commandment. What then means He? Cleave unto them that fear YHUH, who walk in His commandments, which they have received in their hearts; unto them that speak of the ordinances of YHUH, and observe them, unto them who know that the practice of them is a work of gladness, and who meditate on the word of YHUH.

But what means that which cleaves the hoof? It means that the just/tzadik walks even in this world, and expects the holy chayim/life. Behold how well Moshe has made these Torot/laws;

12  But how was it possible for them to perceive, or understand these things? But we, having rightly understood the commandments/mitzvoth, and speak them even as YHUH has willed. On this account has He circumcised our ears and hearts, that we should understand these things.

_____

## Barnabas-Bar-Nava 11

1  Let us inquire, therefore, if YHUH cared to show us beforehand concerning the water and concerning the execution stake. Concerning the water it is written, with respect to Yisrael, how that they will not receive the baptism/mikvah that brings remission of sins, but will establish one for themselves.

2  The prophet therefore speaks in this way, Be astonished, O heavens! And let the earth be afraid still more at this, because this people have done two great and evil things: they have abandoned Me who am the fountain of chayim, and have dug for themselves broken cisterns.

3  Is my holy mountain of Tzion a deserted rock? You shall be as the young of a bird, which has flown when the nest has been taken away.

4  And again the prophet said, I will go before you and will lay low the mountains. And I will break the doors of brass and burst the bars of iron; and I will give unto you the treasures of darkness hidden and unseen, that they may know that I am YHUH Elohim; and, he shall dwell in the lofty cave of the strong rock.

5  Then what says he of the Son? His water is faithful. You shall behold the King in His glory, and your soul shall practice the reverence of YHUH.

6  And again, in another prophet, he said, He that does these things shall be as a tree that grows beside the water, which gives its fruit in its season; and his leaf shall not fall off, and whatever he does shall prosper.

7  Not so are the unrighteous, not so; they are like the dust which the wind carries away from the face of the earth, wherefore the unrighteous shall not rise up in the judgment, nor sinners in the congregation of the just: for YHUH knows the way of the just, but the way of the unrighteous shall perish.

8  You perceive how He has put together the water and the

execution stake. For what He means is this, Blessed are they who having hoped on the execution stake have gone down into the water. For He speaks of a reward to be given at the due season; then, said He, I will render what is due unto you. But now in that He said, Their leaves shall not fall off or go astray, He means this, That every word that goes out from your mouth in emunah/faith and love shall be for a refuge and a hope unto many.

9   And again another prophet said, And the land of Yaakov/Jacob was praised beyond the whole earth. By so saying He means this, He shall glorify the vessel that contains His Ruach.
And what says He afterwards? There was a river flowing on the right, and there grew up on its banks fair trees, and whosoever eats of them shall live forever.

10   By this He means that we go down into the water full of sin and pollution, and go up bearing fruit in the heart, having in the Ruach reverence and hope towards Yahusha. And whoever shall eat of the fair trees shall live forever. He means this, Whoever, He said, shall hear these words spoken and believes them, shall live forever.

---

## Barnabas-Bar-Nava 12

1   In like manner again He signifies concerning the execution stake in another prophet, who said, And when shall these things be fulfilled? YHUH said, When the tree has been bent and shall rise up again, and when blood shall flow from the tree. You have again a prophecy concerning the execution stake and about Him who is about to be crucified.

2   And He said again in Moshe, when Yisrael was being made war upon by foreigners, even that He might remind them while they were being made war upon, that for their sins they were being delivered over unto death; the Ruach said unto the heart of Moshe, that he should make the form of an execution stake, and of Him who was about to suffer.

For He says, If they shall not hope upon Him, they will be made war against forever. Moshe, therefore, arranges weapon against weapon in the midst of the battle, and standing higher than all, stretched out his hands, and so again Yisrael conquered; then, when he let the hands down, they were again slaughtered.

3   Why? That they might know that they are not to be saved except they hope upon Him.

4   And again, in another prophet, he said, All day long have I stretched out my hands unto a people who are disobedient, and who speak against my righteous way.

5   Again, Moshe makes another type of Yahusha, that it behooves that He should suffer, and cause others to live, whom they thought that they had destroyed in figure when Yisrael was falling: For YHUH made every kind of serpent to bite them, and they died, since the transgression happened to Chava/Eve by means of the serpent, to the end that He might convince them that through their transgression they should be given over to the cords of death.

6   For in the end Moshe himself, after he had given a commandment that there shall not be among you a molten image, or a graven image for an elohim, made one himself, that he might

show a type of Yahusha. Moshe, therefore, makes a brazen serpent, and sets it aloft, and calls the people by a proclamation.

7   When, therefore, they had come together they besought Moshe, that he should offer supplication for them concerning their healing. Moshe therefore said unto them, When any of you is bitten, let him come unto the dead serpent, that is placed upon the tree, and let him believe and hope that, though it is dead, it is able to make him live, and immediately he shall be saved; and so they did. You have, therefore, again in these things also, the glory of Yahusha that in Him and to Him are all things.

8   What again said Moshe unto Yahoshua/Joshua the son of Nun, after he had given this name to him, being a prophet? To this end alone, that all the people might hear that the Father reveals all things concerning the Son Yahusha.

9   Moshe therefore said unto Yahoshua the son of Nun, having given him this name, when he sent him to spy out the land, Take the book into your hands and write what YHUH said, even that the Son of Elohim, in the last days, will cut off the whole House of Amalek from the roots.

10   Behold, therefore, again Yahusha, not the son of man, but the Son of Elohim, and by a type made manifest in the flesh. Since, therefore, they should one day say that Messiah is the son of David, David himself prophesies, being in reverence and understanding the deceitfulness of sinners, YHUH said unto my Adon/Master, Sit on my right hand until I make your enemies your footstool.

11   And again Isaiah/Yeshayahu speaks in this way, YHUH said unto Messiah, my YHUH, whose right hand I have held, that the nations should listen before Him, and I will break the strength of kings. Behold how David calls him YHUH, and does not call Him my son.

---

## Barnabas-Bar-Nava 13

1   Let us inquire, therefore, whether this people, or the first people inherit all things, and whether the covenant is for us or for them.

2   Hear, now, what the Scripture said concerning the people. But Yitzchak/Isaac prayed for Rivkah/Rebecca his wife because she was barren, and she conceived. Then went forth Rivkah/Rebecca to inquire of YHUH, and YHUH said unto her, Two nations are in your womb, and two peoples are in your bowels, and the one people shall surpass the other, and the elder shall serve the younger.

3   We ought to understand who was Yitzchak/Isaac and who was Rivkah/Rebecca, and concerning whom He declared that the one people was greater than the other.

4   And in another prophecy Yaakov/Jacob speaks yet more clearly to Yoseph/Joseph his son, saying, Behold YHUH has not deprived me of your face; bring unto me your sons, that I may bless them.

5   And Yoseph brought unto him Ephraim and Manasseh, wishing that he should bless Manasseh, because he was the elder. Yoseph/Joseph, therefore, brought him to the right hand of his father Yaakov/Jacob. But Yaakov/Jacob saw in ruach a figure of the people that should be hereafter.

And what said the Scriptures? And Yaakov/Jacob crossed his hands, and placed his right hand on the head of Ephraim, the second and youngest, and blessed him. And Yoseph/Joseph said unto Yaakov/Jacob, Change your right hand unto the head of Manasseh, because he is my firstborn son. And Yaakov/Jacob said unto Yoseph/Joseph, I know, my child, I know; but the elder shall serve the younger; but this one also shall be blessed.

6   Behold in what way he appointed that this people should be the first and heir of the covenant.

7   If, therefore, it were moreover mentioned through Avraham also, we have the perfecting of our knowledge. What, therefore,

said He unto Avraham, when he alone believed, and it was counted unto him for righteousness? Behold I have made you, Avraham, an abba/father of the nations who in uncircumcision believe in YHUH.

_____

## Barnabas-Bar-Nava 14

1   Yes, but let us inquire whether He has given the covenant that He swear unto the ahvot/fathers that He would give unto the people. Verily He has given it; but they were not worthy to receive it on account of their sins.

2   For the prophet said, And Moshe was fasting on Mount Sinai forty days and forty nights that he might receive the covenant that YHUH has made with His people. And he received from YHUH the two tables that were written in the Ruach/Spirit with the finger of the hand of YHUH. And Moshe, when he had received them, was bringing them down to the people to give it to them.

3   And YHUH said unto Moshe, Moshe, Moshe, get down quickly, for your people, whom you brought out of the land of Mitzrayim/Egypt, have done unlawfully. And Moshe perceived that they had again made molten images, and he cast the tablets from his hands, and the tablets of the covenant of YHUH were broken.

4   Moshe indeed received them, but the people were not worthy. Listen therefore, how we have received them. Moshe received them being a servant, but YHUH Himself gave it unto us to be a people of inheritance, having suffered for our sake.

5   And He was made manifest, that both they might be made full of their sins, and that we, through him that inherited, might receive the covenant of the Adon Yahusha, who, for this purpose was prepared, that by appearing Himself and redeeming our hearts from darkness, which were already lavished on death, and given over to the iniquity of deceit, He might place in us the covenant of His people.

6   For it is written how the Father gives a commandment unto Him, that having redeemed us from darkness, He should prepare for himself a kadosh/holy people.

7   Therefore the prophet said, I, YHUH your Elohim, have called you in righteousness, and I will hold Your hand and make You strong; and I have given You for a covenant to the nation of

Yisrael, for a Light unto the nations also, to open the eyes of the blind, and to bring out of chains them that are bound, and from the house of prison, those that sit in darkness. We know from where we were redeemed.

8   And again, the prophet said, Behold, I have placed You for a light unto the nations that you should be for My Yahusha/salvation even unto the ends of the earth; thus said YHUH Elohim who has redeemed you.

9   And again, the prophet said, The Ruach of YHUH is upon Me, because He has anointed Me to preach the Besorah/gospel unto the poor, He has sent Me to heal those that are broken in heart, to preach deliverance to the captives, and the recovery of sight to the blind, to tell of the acceptable year of YHUH, and the day of recompense, to comfort all that mourn.

_____

## Barnabas-Bar-Nava 15

1  And, moreover, concerning the Shabbat it is written in the Ten Commandments in which He spoke on Mount Sinai unto Moshe face to face: Sanctify the Shabbat of YHUH with pure hands and a pure heart.

2  And in another place He said, If my sons shall keep My Shabbat, then will I place My mercy upon them.

3  He speaks, too, of the Shabbat in the beginning of the creation: And Elohim made in six days the works of His hands, and finished them on the seventh day, and rested on it and sanctified it.

4  Consider, my children, what significance have these words; He finished them in six days. They mean this: that in six thousand years, YHUH will make an end of all things; for a day is with Him is as a thousand years. And He himself bears witness unto me, saying: Behold this day; a day shall be as a thousand years. Therefore, my children, in six days, that is in six thousand years, shall all things be brought to an end.

5  And the words, He rested on the seventh day, have this significance: After that his Son has come, and has caused to cease the time of the wicked one, and has judged the unrighteous, and changed the sun and the moon and the stars, then shall He rest well on the seventh day.

6  And further He said, You shall sanctify it with pure hands and a pure heart. Who, therefore, can sanctify the day that YHUH has sanctified, unless he is pure of heart? In all things have we been deceived.

7  Behold, that then indeed we shall be able to rest well and sanctify; even when we ourselves, having been justified, and having received the promise, when iniquity exists no longer, but all things have been made new by YHUH, we shall then be able to sanctify it, having been first sanctified ourselves.

8  And, furthermore, He said unto them, Your new moons and your Shabbats I cannot endure. See, now, what He means. The

Shabbats, that now are, are not acceptable unto me, but that which I have made is, even that in which, after that I have brought all things to an end, I shall make a beginning of the eighth day, which thing is the beginning of another world the olam haba.

9  Wherefore we keep the eighth day as a day of gladness, on which also Yahusha was discovered risen from the dead, and after which He had appeared ascended unto heaven.

---

## Barnabas-Bar-Nava 16

1   And I will, moreover, tell you concerning the Temple, how these wretched men, being deceived, placed their hopes in the building as if it were the habitation of Elohim, and not on the Elohim who has made them.

2   For almost after the manner of the nations did they consecrate Him in the Temple. But what said YHUH, when making it of no affect? Listen! Who has measured out the heavens with His palm, or the earth with the flat of His hand, is it not I says YHUH? Heaven is My throne, and earth the footstool of My feet. What house will you build for Me, or what shall be the place of My rest? You have known that their hope was vain.

3   And, yet further, He said again, Behold they that have destroyed this Temple shall rebuild it.

4   And so does it happen, for through their war it has been destroyed by the enemy, and now both they themselves and the servants of their enemies shall rebuild it.

5   And again it was made manifest how the Temple and the people of Yisrael should be given up to their enemies. For the Scripture said, And it shall come to pass in the last days that YHUH shall deliver up the sheep of His pasture, and their fold and their tower shall He give up to destruction; and it happened according to that which YHUH had spoken.

6   Let us inquire, therefore, whether there is any Temple of Elohim. There is; even where He himself has declared that He would make and perfect it. For it is written, And it shall be when the week is completed that the Temple of Elohim shall be built gloriously in the name of YHUH.

7   I find, therefore, that there is a Temple; how then shall it be built in the name of YHUH? Learn! Before we believed in Elohim the habitation of our heart was corrupted and feeble, a temple built by our own hands. For it was full of idolatry, and was a habitation of devils, because we did such things as were contrary to Elohim;

8   But it shall be built in the name of YHUH. Pay attention, so that the Temple of YHUH may be built gloriously. But in what manner will it be built? Listen: having received the remission of our sins, and having hoped upon the name of YHUH, we have become new, having been again created entirely. Wherefore Elohim truly dwells in us as a habitation.

9   How? The word of His emunah, the calling of His promise, the wisdom of His Torah-ordinances, the mitzvoth-commandments of His doctrine, He Himself prophesying in us, He himself dwelling in us. To us, who were enslaved by death, He opens the gate of the Temple, which is His mouth, and, giving us repentance, leads us into the incorruptible Temple.

10   For he who desires to be saved looks not unto man, but unto Him that dwells in him and speaks in him, wondering that he had never before heard Him speaking such words out of his own mouth, or even desired to hear them. This is the spiritual Temple built by YHUH.

## Barnabas-Bar-Nava 17

1   So far as it is possible for me to show you these things with simplicity, my mind and soul hope that I have not omitted any of the things that pertain unto salvation;

2   For if I write unto you concerning the things that are at hand, or the things that will be hereafter, you would not be able to understand them, because they are couched in parables. These simple things, therefore, I have written.

―――――――――――――――

## Barnabas-Bar-Nava 18

1   Let us pass on now to another kind of knowledge and instruction. There are two paths of instruction and authority – the one that of Light, and the other that of darkness. But there is a great difference between the two paths. For over the one are appointed as illuminators the malachim/angels of Elohim, over the other the malachim/angels of s.a.tan.

2   On the one side is He who is YHUH, from everlasting to everlasting, on the other is the ruler of the world that now lies in wickedness.

_____

## Barnabas-Bar-Nava 19

1  Now, the path of chayim is this: If any one wishes to travel to the appointed place, let him hasten it by means of his works. Now, the knowledge of walking in it that is given unto us is of this kind:

2  You shall love Him that made you, you shall fear Him that formed you, and you shall glorify Him that redeemed you from death. You shall be simple in heart, and rich in ruach; you shall not cleave unto them that go in the path of death. You shall hate whatever is not pleasing unto Elohim; you shall hate all hypocrisy; you shall not abandon the mitzvoth- commandments of YHUH;

3  You shall not exalt yourself; you shall be humble in all things; you shall not take glory for yourself; you shall not take evil counsel against your neighbor; you shall not take audacity into your soul.

4  You shall not commit fornication, you shall not commit adultery. You shall not pollute yourself with mankind: let not the Word of Elohim go forth from you in corruption. You shall not accept the person of any to reprove any man for transgression. You shall be gentle, you shall be quiet; you shall tremble at the words that you have heard; you shall not bear malice against your brother;

5  You shall not doubt whether a thing shall be or not; you shall not take the name of YHUH in vain. You shall love your neighbor beyond your own soul; you shall not kill a child by abortion, neither shall you destroy it after it is born. You shall not remove your hand from your son or your daughter, but shall teach them from their youth the fear of YHUH.

6  You shall not covet your neighbor's goods; you shall not be an extortioner; you shall not cleave with your soul unto the proud, but you shall have your conversation with the lowly and the just. Receive as blessings the troubles that come unto you, knowing that without Elohim nothing happens.

7  You shall not be double-minded nor double-tongued, for to be

double- tongued is the snare of death. You shall submit yourself to your teachers- masters as to the image of Elohim, with shame and fear. You shall not give commands with bitterness to your servant and your handmaid, who hopes in the same Elohim as you do, lest, perchance, you cease to reverence Elohim, who is over both. For He [Yahusha] came not to call men with respect of persons, but to call those whom the Ruach had prepared.

8   You shall communicate in all things with your neighbor, and shall not say that things are your own. For if you are partners in that which is incorruptible, how much more in the things that are corruptible? You shall not be hasty of speech, for the mouth is a snare of death. As far as you are able, you shall be pure concerning your soul.

9   Be not a stretcher forth of your hand in receiving, but drawer back of it in giving. You shall love, as the apple of your eye, every one that speaks unto you the Word of YHUH.

10   You shall remember the Day of Judgment by night and by day; and you shall seek out every day the persons of the kiddushim-saints.

11   You shall not doubt to give, nor shall you murmur in giving. Give to everyone that asks you, and then you shall know who is the tov/good Recompenser of the reward. You shall take care of that which you have received, neither adding to it, nor taking from it. You shall hate the evil man unto the end, and shall judge justly.

12   You shall not make a schism, but shall make shalom by bringing adversaries together. You shall make confession of your sins. You shall not go unto prayer with an evil conscience. This is the way of chayim; laboring by means of the Word and proceeding to exhort, and practicing to save the soul by the Word, or you shall work by your hands for the redemption of your sins.

———————————————

## Barnabas-Bar-Nava 20

1   But the path of darkness is crooked and full of cursing, for it is the path of eternal death and punishment, in which way the things are that destroy the soul. Idolatry, boldness, the pride of power, hypocrisy, double-heartedness, adultery, murder, rape, haughtiness, transgression, deceit, malice, self-will, witchcraft, sorcery, covetousness, lack of the reverence of Elohim.

2   These are they who are persecutors of the tov/good, haters of truth, lovers of lies; they who know not the reward of righteousness, who cleave not to what is tov/good nor unto just judgment; who attend not to the widow and the orphan; who are awake not unto the reverence of Elohim, but unto evil; from whom meekness and patience are far off; who love the things that are vain, who follow after recompense, who pity not the poor, who labor not for him who is in trouble; who are prompt to evil-speaking, who know not Him that made them; murderers of children, corruptors of the image of Elohim; who turn away from the poor man and oppress the afflicted; advocates of the rich, unjust judges of the poor, sinners in all things.

---

## Barnabas-Bar-Nava 21

1  It is therefore right that he who has learned the Torah ordinances of YHUH, even as many as have been written beforehand, should walk in them. For he who does these things shall be glorified in the kingdom of Elohim, but he who chooses the contrary things shall perish together with his works. On this account is the resurrection; on this account is the retribution.

2  I ask those who are of high estate among you, if you will receive any friendly advice from me; keep those with you toward whom you may do what is honorable. Fail not in so doing.

3  The day is at hand in which everything shall perish together with the evil one, YHUH is near at hand and His reward also.

4  Again and again do I ask you, be tov/good lawgivers over yourselves, be you tov/good advisers of yourselves. Abide faithful counselors of one another; take out of the midst of you all hypocrisy,
5  And may Elohim, who rules the whole olam/world, give you wisdom, understanding, science, knowledge of His ordinances, and patience.

6  And be taught of Elohim, inquiring what YHUH seeks of you and so do that work that you may be found saved in the Day of Judgment.

7  But if there is any memory of that which is tov/good, remember me while you practice these things, so that both your desire and your watching over it may turn unto some tov/good.

8  I beseech you this, asking it as a favor. So long as the tov/good vessel is with you, fail not in any of these things, but seek them out without ceasing, and fulfill all the Torah commandments, for these things are worthy.

9  Therefore I have been very anxious to write unto you, so far as I was able, to the end that I might make you glad. Farewell, children of love and shalom; the Elohim of glory and of all

unmerited favor be with your ruach. Omein.

*May His Malchut-Kingdom Grow In You!*

Made in the USA
Columbia, SC
27 September 2024

43171564R00026